D0499068

BLACK DAISIES FOR THE BRIDE

by the same author

Plays

THE MYSTERIES
THE TRACKERS OF OXYRHYNCHUS
THE COMMON CHORUS
SQUARE ROUNDS

Poetry

THE LOINERS
PALLADAS: POEMS
FROM THE SCHOOL OF ELOQUENCE AND OTHER POEMS
CONTINUOUS
A KUMQUAT FOR JOHN KEATS
U.S. MARTIAL
SELECTED POEMS
THE FIRE-GAP
V.
A COLD COMING
THE GAZE OF THE GORGON

Theatre

DRAMATIC VERSE
THEATRE WORKS

BLACK DAISIES
FOR THE BRIDE

TONY HARRISON

faber and faber
LONDON · BOSTON

First published in Great Britain in 1993
by Faber and Faber Limited
3 Queen Square London WC1N 3AU

Photoset by Parker Typesetting Service, Leicester
Printed by Clays Ltd, St Ives plc

Photographs of Muriel Allen (facing Musical Note)
and Kathleen Dickenson (facing page 1),
© Geoff Franklin, 1993

A CIP record for this book
is available from the British Library.

ISBN 0-571-17129-X

2 4 6 8 10 9 7 5 3 1

To
the staff and residents of Whernside Ward

Black Daisies for the Bride was first broadcast on 30 June on BBC2.

THERAPIST	Elaine Hallam
YOUNG MARIA	Maria Bovino
YOUNG KATHLEEN	Cathryn Bradshaw
YOUNG MURIEL	Maria Friedman
HOSPITAL ENTERTAINER	Richard Muttonchops
Music	Dominic Muldowney
Director	Peter Symes
Producer	Fiona Finlay
Camera	Mike Fox, John Daly
Editor	Peter Simpson
Researcher	Harriet Bakewell

STAFF OF WHERNSIDE WARD, HIGH ROYDS HOSPITAL

DAY: John Tennison (Acting Senior Charge Nurse); Steve Toal (Charge Nurse); Bob Moran (Acting Charge Nurse); Angela Fielding (Senior Staff Nurse); Robert Maginnis (Senior Staff Nurse); Liz Young (Staff Nurse); Irene Kirk (Enrolled Nurse); Mand Morland (EN); Kamla Suarez (EN); Maria Withy; Joan Ambler; Peter Stott; Rita Jefferson; Sarah Haley; Christine Miller; Pilar Haney; Sheila Brown; Audrey Robinson; Heather Dalton; Christina Acebal; Olive Watson

NIGHT: Denis Stanley (EN); Anita Johnson (EN); Ann Miller; Jenny Roe; Audrey Wilton; Joyce McIntosh; Pat Renton; Paddy Suraweera

Christine Davey (Cleaner); Joyce Cockroft (Housekeeper)

MUSICAL NOTE

The dialogue and songs in this script are modelled on the
following music:

1.   'Daisy, Daisy, give me your answer do!'
     (Words and music: Harry Dacre)
2.   'Oh! You Beautiful Doll'
     (Music: Nat D. Ayer. Words: A. Seymour Brown)
3.   '*Vogliatemi bene*' from Act I, *Madama Butterfly*, by Puccini.
4.   'In the Bleak Mid-Winter' (arr: Holst).

In the script the following abbreviations are used to indicate
which model of pre-existing music a particular line follows:

DD = 'Daisy Daisy' (a verse of 6 lines)
BD = 'Beautiful Doll' (a verse of 7 lines)
BMW = 'Bleak Mid-Winter' (a verse of 4 lines)

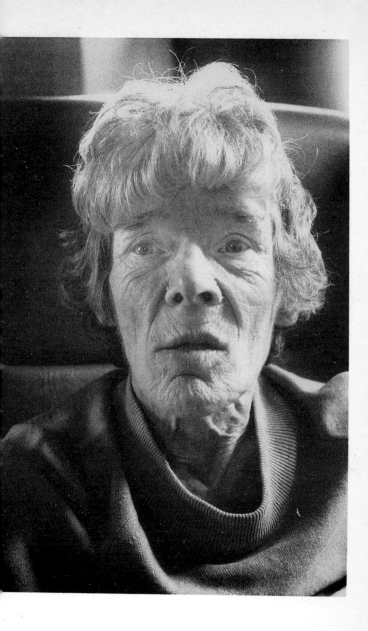

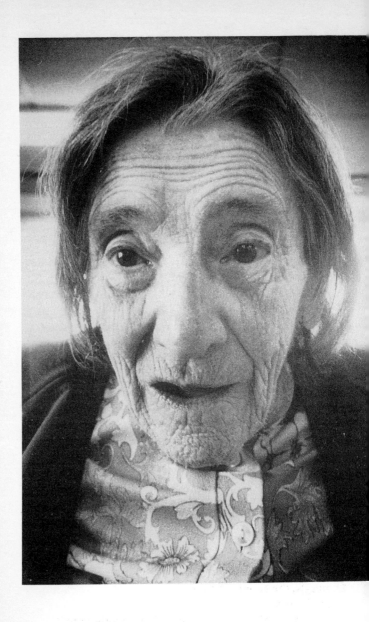

I. EXT. HIGH ROYDS HOSPITAL, DAY
A Yorkshire dry-stone wall. The clock tower of High Royds Hospital,
Menston, near Ilkley, is first glimpsed through a crack in the dry-stone
wall, then seen in the distance as the central feature of a large
Victorian psychiatric hospital, opened in 1888 as the West Yorkshire
Paupers' Lunatic Asylum.
   Soundtrack: a recording from c. 1950 of MARIA TOBIN *singing*
'Vogliatemi bene' *from the end of Act I of* Madama Butterfly, *in an*
English translation:
   'Ah, love me a little,
   Oh just a very little,
   As you would love a baby.
   'Tis all that I ask for . . .'
Old recording fades down on high note, and MARIA TOBIN, *the*
resident of Whernside Ward, 1992, fades up singing what might be
regarded as her one surviving note from 'Madama Butterfly'.

2. INT. WHERNSIDE WARD, HIGH ROYDS HOSPITAL, DAY
Beginning with MARIA TOBIN, *five residents of Whernside Ward, all*
victims of Alzheimer's disease in its various stages, address us directly,
like news-readers or storytellers, but in their own form of progressively
disintegrating English. They are:
   MARIA TOBIN (*b.* 1912)
   DOROTHY CHAPLIN (*b.* 1927)
   with MURIEL ALLEN (*b.* 1927) *in the background*
   MURIEL PRIOR (*b.* 1913)
   IRENE CLEMENTS (*b.* 1920)
   KATHLEEN DICKENSON (*b.* 1908)

MARIA TOBIN
   O murals, the babble of ewes,
   beautiful Jews.
   I said 'Oo . . . Mm . . . I'll come and buy another two.'
   (*Laughs.*)

He said, 'Everything is right!'
I said, 'Oo, that's good!'
Yes, it would be better.
It's nicer when they come in
and they're not worrying all the day.

DOROTHY CHAPLIN

Oo flippin' 'eck it . . . it's like . . .
Oo 'eck . . . 'eckykyeck.
And then . . .
t'bloomin' clegs have to come a down a bit
and, er . . .
(Claps.)
Oh get down stairs, them . . . them bloody steps!
(Laughs.)
(MURIEL ALLEN *drums her feet rhythmically in the background.*)

MURIEL PRIOR

I love you!
I love you!
I love you!
I love you!

IRENE CLEMENTS

The only poory, poory, poory, poory
lickit in the Andes.
Take it over they're playing it then
(Laughs. MARIA TOBIN'*s one note is heard.*)
Come alongdong then, darling doggy!
Dindin, and you'll gettyget.

KATHLEEN DICKENSON

*(Utters stream of untranscribable consonants and vowels,
apparently meaningless but with much of the intention, rhythm and
ghostly structure of communication.)*

3. EXT. HIGH ROYDS HOSPITAL, DAY
A reflected cloud passes through a hospital window.
   Sound track: Maria Tobin's one trilled surviving note from
Madame Butterfly *is gradually obliterated by the distant sound of an
electric tug used for carrying waste and meals down the long hospital
corridors. Its sound is like that of the chilling wind of a gathering*

2

nter storm. Both cloud and tug forebode the blizzard of
getfulness.

INT. WHERNSIDE WARD, DAY
ythmical montage begins with two patients – MABEL FROST,
ting at a table, and GLADYS MIDDLETON, seated – calling out their
aracteristic repetitive cries.

ABEL FROST
Come! Come! Come! Come! Come! . . .
ADYS MIDDLETON
Tell us!

INT. HIGH ROYDS HOSPITAL, MAIN HALL, INTERCUT
TH WHERNSIDE WARD (*continuing montage*)
e THERAPIST arrives through the main door, and walks down tiled
rridor over mosaics of black daisies dating from the earliest period of
hospital.
The THERAPIST's walking rhythm is intercut with patients' cries,
ating hands, feet, the swaying of nurses' watches, etc.

INT. LONG CORRIDOR LEADING TO WHERNSIDE WARD,
Y
e THERAPIST walks the length of the corridor towards Whernside
ard door with its red sign.
An electric hospital tug, carrying yellow and blue waste bags,
ertakes the THERAPIST.
A MALE PATIENT, probably from a ward for schizophrenics,
lks in a black raincoat down the long corridor, smoking. His clouds
smoke hang in slanting shafts of sunlight.
The THERAPIST passes a seated WOMAN PATIENT sitting on one
the fold-down seats provided in the long corridor. The WOMAN
TIENT *takes a puff from a cigarette in her right hand. The* WOMAN
TIENT *takes a puff from a cigarette in her left hand.*
The THERAPIST approaches the door of Whernside Ward.

INT. WHERNSIDE WARD, DAY
e THERAPIST arrives and is greeted by MARIA TOBIN singing her

3

'*one note out of* Butterfly'.

MARIA TOBIN (*Voice over*)
    But it has to be told!
    (*The* THERAPIST *and* MARIA TOBIN *walk together towards*
    Nursing Office, with MARIA TOBIN *again giving voice to her note*

8. INT. WHERNSIDE WARD NURSING OFFICE, DAY
The THERAPIST *greets Senior Charge Nurse* JOHN TENNISON *in th*
Nursing Office. They look at the board of residents' names and discus
one of them, namely MURIEL ALLEN.
    Close-up: name board and name: MURIEL ALLEN.
    They turn and look out of the window of the Nursing Office on to
the ward.

9. INT. WHERNSIDE WARD
The THERAPIST *sings 'Daisy, Daisy' to* MURIEL ALLEN.
    MURIEL ALLEN *stops her repetitive moans and listens briefly, but*
does not respond.

THERAPIST (*Sings*)
    Daisy, Daisy, give me your answer do!
    I'm half crazy all for the love of you!
    It won't be a stylish marriage,
    I can't afford a carriage,
    But you'll look sweet upon the seat
    Of a bicycle made for two.

    Daisy, Daisy . . .
    (*The* THERAPIST *tails off in disappointment.*)

11. INT. WHERNSIDE WARD, DAY
MURIEL ALLEN, *having disengaged herself from the efforts of the*
THERAPIST, *wanders within reach of the seated* ELEANOR
BELLERBY, *who makes to grab her.*

12. INT. WHERNSIDE WARD, NURSING OFFICE, DAY
The THERAPIST *sits in the office with* JOHN TENNISON.

THERAPIST [DD 6]
She sang Daisy two weeks ago!
(JOHN TENNISON *looks from his work to the* THERAPIST, *acknowledging the disappearance of the very last song in Muriel Allen's dwindled repertoire. He then hears a scream from* MURIEL ALLEN *being attacked by* ELEANOR BELLERBY *outside the Nursing Office.* JOHN TENNISON *leaves to deal with the fracas.*)

3. INT. WHERNSIDE WARD, DAY

JOHN TENNISON [DD 1a]
Ladies! Ladies!

4. INT. NURSING OFFICE, DAY
The THERAPIST *looks out at* JOHN TENNISON *separating the squabbling women.*

THERAPIST (*Voice over*) [DD 1b, 2]
                  Thinking what they've all been
  makes Alzheimer's horrible . . . obscene.

5. INT. WHERNSIDE WARD
Wordless music. [DD 3, 4]   MARIA TOBIN *sings her 'one note out of Butterfly'.*

6. INT. NURSING OFFICE
JOHN TENNISON, *returning from separating the two women, pauses to register Maria Tobin's note, and offers it as some comfort to the disappointed* THERAPIST.

JOHN TENNISON [DD 5a]
  She always sings
  (JOHN TENNISON *passes* THERAPIST *and sits at desk.*)
THERAPIST [DD 5b, 6]
                  but everything's
  her one note out of *Butterfly!*
  (MARIA TOBIN *sings her note again.*)
THERAPIST [DD 1–6]
  Listen! Listen! You remember that time before

I tried Maria with the Puccini score.
But every bar that I was playing
had only her one A in,
the one trilled A she sings all day
and she never remembers more.
(*The phone on John Tennison's desk rings.* JOHN TENNISON
answers it.)

JOHN TENNISON [DD 1a]
Whernside! Hold on!
(JOHN TENNISON *places his hand over the receiver and turns to the*
THERAPIST *who is preparing to leave.*)

THERAPIST [DD 1b]
. . . Next session's Muriel Prior.
(*The* THERAPIST *looks through the glass window of the Nursing
Office towards* MURIEL PRIOR *being seated by nurses in the ward.*

THERAPIST (*Voice over, thinking*) [DD 2]
She could be one who music might inspire!

JOHN TENNISON [DD 3–6]
With Christmas about to happen
we've got that banjo chap 'n
he might get through with one or two.
After him there's St Mary's choir.
(JOHN TENNISON *turns back, takes his hand off the receiver, and
speaks to his caller.*
The THERAPIST *leaves the Nursing Office.*)

17. INT. WHERNSIDE WARD, ENTRANCE CORRIDOR, DAY
The THERAPIST *presses the four numbers on the electronic access
security pad that operates the door out of Whernside Ward into the long
hospital corridor.*
*Close-up of the digits 6288, the numbers which open the door. The
four numbers are synchronized to the first four notes of the tune of
'Daisy, Daisy', which forms the basis of the Therapist's Song. The
door opens.*

THERAPIST (*Voice over, speaking on opening door*)
(6 . . . 2 . . . 8 . . . 8) Today brought me no success!
(*The door slams behind the* THERAPIST *and her song begins.*)

6

INT. LONG HOSPITAL CORRIDOR, DAY

The THERAPIST *walks down the corridor singing the Therapist's song, exiting over the entrance hall mosaic of black daisies, with the main door finally slamming behind her.*

She passes the MALE PATIENT *in black raincoat making a phone call on the corridor payphone.*

THE THERAPIST'S SONG

[6 ... 2 ... 8 ... 8] Today brought me no success!
Muriel Allen stayed locked in her deep distress.
The monstrous misadventure
of Alzheimer's dementia
has struck one who, who used to do . . .
well, what *did* she do, try and guess?

Muriel Allen, a therapist like me
now beyond all forms of therapy.
And if Alzheimer's doesn't spare a
lifetime professional carer,
and destroys a mind of Muriel's kind,
and a therapist . . . no one's free!

Muriel Allen's days have all gone astray,
life's bright blossoms clutched in one black bouquet.
The music in her still lingers
in twisting, twitching fingers,
and in the beat of sneakered feet
that she drums in the ward all day.

Daisies! Daisies! Their petals black and thrown,
thrown on paths where memories turn to stone.
A black bouquet of these is
for brides Alzheimer's seizes.
The groom beside each white-clad bride
wears a black daisy buttonhole . . .

19. EXT. HIGH ROYDS HOSPITAL, MAIN DOOR

A yellow sign reads PLEASE KEEP THESE DOORS SHUT. *The*
THERAPIST *exits past the sign with the door slamming behind her,*
cutting off the last note of her song. She stops to savour the world
outside the hospital beneath a black sign which reads WELCOME TO
HIGH ROYDS HOSPITAL. *She looks at the bare winter trees with*
rooks' nests in their branches, suggesting the pattern of the brain's
blood supply with the sections damaged, as an Alzheimer's patient's
brain might be revealed through positron emission tomography. An
X-Ray of forgetfulness.

   In the Therapist's mind a choir of schoolchildren begin to sing to a
tune based on 'In the Bleak Mid-Winter'.

CHOIR [BMW 3]
   Songs seem last to leave the brain, leave the brain.
   (*The* THERAPIST *crosses to her car parked outside the dormitory of*
   Whernside Ward. We see reflections of the leafless trees in the
   window of the ward and the shape of a hospital iron bedstead. She
   pauses by the open door of her car and looks again at the bare
   brainscan trees on the horizon.)
THERAPIST (*Voice over, speaking*) [BMW 4a]
   But in Muriel Allen . . .
   (*The* THERAPIST *gets into her car and, when she is seated, sings*
   [BMW 4b]:)
                        . . . none remain!
(*Soundtrack: the sound of a hospital electric tug moving down the*
long corridor, like the sound of an ominous wind. It is the beginning
of the blizzard of forgetfulness. The blizzard starts with a few flakes
of wedding confetti in the shapes of bells, hearts, loveknots and
horseshoes of various colours falling onto the windscreen of the
therapist's car.)
CHOIR (*Voice over*) [BMW 3, 4]
   All life's brightest moments filling hearts and heads,
   Alzheimer's, like a blizzard, rips up into shreds.

9

(The blizzard of confetti builds in intensity, obliterating the therapist's view of the outside world. As the blizzard intensifies we hear more sounds of the electric tug passing down the corridor and the voices of the CHORUS OF RELATIVES *of residents of Whernside Ward recollecting the first stages of the Alzheimer's disease which afflicts their loved ones. She switches on the windscreen-wipers, whose rhythm recalls the rhythmical montage which first introduced us to the hospital.)*

CHORUS OF RELATIVES
It takes everything away from you, dun't it?
It's the stripping away of all present memory.
The person that you knew is no longer there, but the shell is there.
He put his pants on back to front.
Auntie got doubly incontinent.
He couldn't find even simple words for *Scrabble*.
He started ringing me up in the night.
He was always getting lost.
He couldn't sign his name; he couldn't write or anything.
Apple cores in vases, stuck amongst plants.
He was aggressive with his own reflection.
All the ornaments started being painted gold.
It's like a bereavement.
It *is* a bereavement. It's horrible.
She started being lonely and she started losing things, hiding
    things and forgetting things.
She put her windscreen-washer on when I said indicate.
She got a pair of scissors and just cut through an electric cable.

20. INT. WHERNSIDE WARD NURSING OFFICE, DAY
The WARD CLEANER *with the same rhythm as the windscreen-wipers erases writing from the board where the residents' names are listed. A* NURSE *(who we will later see singing as the young bride* MARIA TOBIN*) writes in a space in the list of names the name* MARIA TOBIN *in red marker ink.*

CHORUS OF RELATIVES *(Voice over)*
    (The sister, brother and daughter of Maria Tobin)
    My mother could put a dress together in two minutes, absolutely

fabulous, she was a fantastic woman.
The way she made friends was amazing.
She helped people who were in trouble, she comforted them.

21. INT. WHERNSIDE WARD, DAY

MARIA TOBIN *seated in a chair beneath a decoration of white plastic roses and lilies of the valley.*

MARIA TOBIN
We're all happy, we're all knotting.
I went in the other day and pushed the . . .
. . . my knitwell for the two . . .
two men and the bends at the back,
that were dying, crying, almost crying . . .
Christ had said to him, 'You're mine!'
and I put the receiver on.
He'd made it all himself.
I didn't like it at all.
And then the Queen Mary came up and sat on top of me.
I went down to see her, and she said . . .
mmm . . .
(*Imitating Queen Mary.*)
'Oh hello dear, how are you?
How are you? Can you help me?'
So I said, 'Well, what are you selling for?'
He says, 'I am charging a change of heel . . .
of *heel*!'
You've got to watch your watch as . . . as stead.
So this poor lad had to wait . . .
wait for his lotchester.
So I went and locked it in,
left it in, and he came in.
He just had it in today.
I put it on my head.
(*Laughs.*)
I said, 'Oo God! I can't lose my lids now.'
(*Touches hair as if to prepare herself for some important occasion.*)
I'm going to get all my colls today,

Yes, milk core . . . milk call and my crepe silk paws.
(*She hears her young self singing 'Ah, love me a little' from*
Madame Butterfly. *She sighs.*)
Cosi fai?
Che besogna?
(*The camera tilts from* MARIA TOBIN *up to the bouquet of white*
plastic roses and lilies of the valley.
    Mix to:)

22. ROSTRUM CAMERA SHOT

Rostrum camera shot of the wedding photograph of MARIA TOBIN.
The bride carries a bouquet identical to the arrangement of white
plastic roses and lilies of the valley in the ward.

  The photograph is seen through the mesh of the window of the door
out of Whernside Ward, framed by the cream-coloured door. To the
right of the window a blue and white circular sign reads FIRE DOOR
KEEP SHUT. *The camera pulls focus from the window mesh to* MARIA
TOBIN *in all her bridal glory.*

  Soundtrack: the Puccini aria in the young Maria Tobin's recording
continues.

23. INT. ENTRANCE CORRIDOR, WHERNSIDE WARD, DAY

The NURSE (*who is to sing as the young bride* MARIA TOBIN) *walks*
towards the door of Whernside Ward and presses the 6288 access code
to exit. As the numbers are pressed, Maria Tobin's song is cued by four
notes synchronized to the nurse's finger on each digit. The song is an
arrangement of the original Puccini aria recorded by the young Maria
Tobin c. 1950.

24. INT. LONG CORRIDOR OUTSIDE WHERNSIDE WARD, DAY

The door opens. The door slams behind the NURSE *who is transformed*
into the young MARIA TOBIN *dressed in all her wedding finery and*
carrying a bouquet of roses and lilies of the valley. Everything about
her appearance matches the original photograph. She begins to sing the
once-familiar but now forgotten Puccini aria, and as she does so she
moves down the corridor, away from the presentiment of her future
residence on Whernside Ward, represented by the voices of nurses in
her head.

THE SONG OF THE BRIDE I
Maria Tobin

MARIA TOBIN
My name's Maria Tobin!
Yes, half of Leeds was gawping and throwing confetti,
ooing that I'm so pretty,
but now the cloud I'm under, dark'ning my mem'ry,
buries my piano with *Butterfly* score on.
(*Following the musical line where Butterfly's lover, B. F.
Pinkerton, responds to her in the original Puccini score, the* VOICES
OF NURSES *are heard cajoling or cautioning* MARIA TOBIN, *the
present resident on Whernside Ward.*)
VOICES OF NURSES (*Voice over*)
Breakfast, Maria, put your pinafore on!
Maria, NO! That's an electric cable!
Sing us a song Maria!
MARIA TOBIN (*Distancing herself from the voices*)
I knew so much Puccini
Bohème and *Butterfly*
Now I've forgotten and my flutt'ring Butterfly's on . . .
on a dark'ning horizon.
VOICE OF NURSE (*Voice over*)
Maria, come and sing!
MARIA TOBIN (*Voice over*)
That bloody 'Daisy' song!
VOICE OF THERAPIST (*Voice over, singing*)
'Give me your answer do.'
MARIA TOBIN (*Voice over*)
My answer's NO then!
That bloody 'Daisy, Daisy!'
MARIA TOBIN
Maria!
I've lost Maria!
Maria!

25. INT. END OF LONG CORRIDOR. AUTOMATIC DOORS
*The young bride searches for her lost self, singing her own name, and
as she approaches the doors marked with blue and yellow signs*
AUTOMATIC DOORS – KEEP CLEAR *they open on to a dark oblivion
through which a blizzard of confetti blows, obliterating the torn poster
on which can still be read* MARIA TOBIN, ITALIAN OPERA STAR.

    *As the automatic doors close they trap the train of the wedding dress,
crushing the silver appliquéd shape of what might be both loveknot or
butterfly. The image recalls the exchange between Madama Butterfly
and Pinkerton on the fragile nature of the butterfly, and Butterfly's
fears of suffering a similar fate to the delicate, pierced creature whose
name she bears:*

  Pinkerton:
    Mia Butterfly
    Come t'han ben nomata
    Tenue farfalla . . .
  Butterfly:
    Dicon ch'oltre mare
    Se cade in man dell'uom
    Ogni farfalla d'uno spillo
    E trafitta
    Ed in tavola infitta!

26. INT. WHERNSIDE WARD, DAY
Darkness on the entrance corridor. It is early morning. The
HOUSEKEEPER, JOYCE COCKCROFT, *switches on a light, and then
another.*

    *Close-up of rows of tea mugs. From a large metal teapot the first of
the mugs are filled.*

    MARIA TOBIN *is given a mug of tea by the* NURSE *(who we have
just seen singing the Song of the Bride I).*

    Another NURSE *gives a mug of tea to another resident.*

    From the door marked FEMALE DORMITORY, *supported by*
NURSES STEVE TOAL *and* MARIA WITHY, MURIEL PRIOR *emerges,*

14

shuffling with difficulty. She is helped to sit at a table.

KATHLEEN DICKENSON *is seated at a table drinking tea.* IRENE CLEMENTS *is seated at a table staring ahead, seemingly lost in concentration. On her left the former therapist* MURIEL ALLEN *is seated and begins to scream in her characteristic way. The* CHOIR *sings throughout.*

CHOIR [BMW 1, 2]
    Muriel Prior's scarcely able still to walk,
    only says 'I love you' if and when she'll talk.

    [BMW 1–4]
    Slowly they're forgetting everything they've been,
    accordionist like Kathleen, crooner like Irene.

    Songs that Irene used to croon, used to croon,
    though the words are garbled still have tune.

    [BMW 1, 2]
    Irene hates such noises, Muriel Allen's shriek,
    they disturb her music fading week by week.

IRENE CLEMENTS (*Sync*)
    Shut up you, you bugger and deggarad.

CHOIR [BMW 1–4]
    Kathleen played piano, played accordion too,
    sometimes her hands remember what they used to do.

    But mostly Kathleen cleans and cleans, cleans and cleans
    as though the home she lives in's still Kathleen's.

    [BMW 1–4]
    And it's bustling Kathleen's most repeated chore
    to wipe and clean and polish Whernside Ward's locked door.
    (KATHLEEN DICKENSON *tries the door and finds it locked.*)

    Kath's caressing fingers coaxed, coaxed accordion chord
    but can't press the door-code that opens Whernside Ward.

(KATHLEEN DICKENSON *spends a good deal of her day bustling energetically around Whernside Ward, cleaning almost every object she comes into contact with, licking her forefinger and index finger, and applying the spittle to the object intended to be cleaned and polished. She is seen going through this daily routine.*)

27. INT. WHERNSIDE WARD NURSING OFFICE, DAY
The WARD CLEANER (*who is to sing the Song of the Bride II*) *writes on the board of residents' names the name* KATHLEEN DICKENSON *in green marker ink.*

CHORUS OF RELATIVES (*Voice over*)
(*Kathleen Dickenson's niece*)
Auntie was very kind and gentle; loved children. Danced with 'em, sang with 'em.
She used to play the piano for 'em, play the accordion for 'em, learn 'em how to knit and crochet.
She used to grow all her own flowers, vegetables. She never bought a vegetable. I don't think there were anything she couldn't do, you know, when she was all right.
She was ever so clever . . . Yes . . . yes . . .

28. INT. WHERNSIDE WARD, DAY
KATHLEEN DICKENSON, *after her seemingly endless cleaning chores, is resting in a chair beneath a shelf with an arrangement of white plastic lilies. She looks up and is apparently thinking. The camera tilts up to the flowers.*
Mix to:

29. ROSTRUM CAMERA SHOT
Rostrum camera shot of the wedding photograph of KATHLEEN DICKENSON *with her husband Harold. The bride carries a bouquet identical to the arrangement of white plastic lilies in the ward.*
The photograph is seen through the mesh of the window of the door out of Whernside Ward, framed by the cream-coloured door. To the right of the window a blue and white circular signs reads FIRE DOOR KEEP SHUT. *The camera pulls focus from the window mesh to the photograph of the married couple.*

30. INT. ENTRANCE CORRIDOR, WHERNSIDE WARD, DAY
A WARD CLEANER *in blue overalls walks towards the door of Whernside Ward and presses the 6288 access code to exit. As the*

umbers are pressed the Song of the Bride II is cued by four notes from
the tune of 'Oh You Beautiful Doll' (Ayer, arr. Muldowney). The
door opens and the blue overall passes through the frame.

. INT. LONG HOSPITAL CORRIDOR
The flaring hem of the cream silk wedding dress of KATHLEEN
DICKENSON, and a pair of white high-heeled shoes, emerge through
the bottom of the open door.
  The door slams shut. KATHLEEN DICKENSON in her wedding dress
begins to sing the Song of the Bride II.
  She moves down the corridor with the kind of energy that is still
apparent in her older self, but her relish and energy are shadowed by a
resentiment of her future and she sees through a corridor window the
continuous blizzard of forgetfulness.

THE SONG OF THE BRIDE II
Kathleen Dickenson

Yeh, a motorbike bride, I'm Kath the motorbike bride.
Harold and me we used to court on
a BSA and then a Norton,
Harold, him steering, and me, me in the car at the side,
motorbiked to mountains, me and Harold went
up Mickle Fell, and up Penyghent,
c . . . c . . . c . . . can't you still tell from my stride?

And together we'd bike to every good mountainous scene.
Wrapped up well in warm windjammers,
gazed at peak-top panoramas,
those long vistas of green, those great long vistas of green.
Climbed up Whernside, Yorkshire's toughest peak,
that out of puff we couldn't speak
(*three breaths*) . . . till Harold said 'I love you, Kathleen!'
'I love you, Kathleen!'
'I love you, Kathleen!'

Nothing, nothing of that, nothing, none of it stays,
motorbiking, mountaineering,
lost in mists I won't see clearing,
lost in the blizzard of days, the burying blizzard of days.
From the Whernside tramped up in our mountain gear
to this Whernside wandered with no Harold here,
and . . . and . . . and . . . those . . . long green vistas all greys.

(*Voice over camera track around* KATHLEEN DICKENSON, *the
present resident on Whernside Ward.*)

. . .
. . .
. . .
. . .

If I hadn't lost the power to reminisce
these are the moments that my heart would miss,
m . . . m . . . m . . . m . . . moments on mountains with him.

(The bride on the corridor drops her bouquet.)

(And my fingers were green, won every gardening prize.
No one's fingers could be greener
than Kathleen's, our restless cleaner.
Feasts for the lips as well as feasts for the eyes –
pies from home-grown rasps, pies from home-grown straws,
pies out of bil'bries off of Ilkley Moors,
g . . . g . . . g . . . garden-grown gooseberry pies!)

If you want to know who, you really want to know who,
who she's been then cast your eyes on
cloth she crocheted butterflies on,
fish Kath caught with her rod, these fruits that Kathleen once
    grew.
Kathleen was, before Alzheimer's cruelly struck,
an angler, climber, dancer, gardener, cook –
now . . . now . . . now . . . now . . . Kath knows nothing she
    knew.

All I remember is four or, at the very most, five
words that still've got some meaning
spending days on Whernside cleaning,
not much memory left, soon even less'll survive.
With Alzheimer's shredding all remembered time,
the blizzard's blowing, but Godammit I'm . . .
g . . . gl . . . gla . . . glad . . . I'm still Kath and alive!
                  I'm still Kath and alive!
                  I'm still Kath and alive!

32. INT. END OF LONG CORRIDOR, AUTOMATIC DOORS

Before the automatic doors, on which can be read the blue and yellow signs reading AUTOMATIC DOORS – KEEP CLEAR, *is set a table covered with a white tablecloth with crocheted butterflies and vine leaves made many years before by the Kathleen Dickenson who is now a resident on Whernside Ward. On the table are laid plates and bowls filled with the products of Kathleen Dickenson's gardening and angling. There is a bowl of raspberries, a bowl of strawberries, some sticks of rhubarb (the most commonly grown fruit in Leeds), a bowl of gooseberries and a number of runner beans. There is a blue plate patterned with butterflies with four trout freshly caught by Kathleen Dickenson herself as a young champion angler. There is a vase of blue and yellow flowers from her garden.*

The bride circles the table, trailing her fingers along the edge of the plate with the fish. Her white-clad reflection passes across the shiny wet bodies of the fish. Her wedding veil snags briefly on a protruding stick of rhubarb.

As a final affirmation of an undiminished relish for existence, the bride, KATHLEEN DICKENSON *picks up the bowl of her home-grown strawberries, and savours their scent and deliciousness. She turns with the bowl and the automatic doors open. They open onto a dark oblivion with a blizzard of confetti. The bride disappears slowly into the darkness swirling with confetti.*

Cut to:

33. INT. WHERNSIDE WARD, DAY

A table with a plastic bowl of strawberry yoghurt and a spoon. The spoon, full of yoghurt and spilling over, is lifted to the mouth of KATHLEEN DICKENSON. *Yoghurt drops from the spoon to the floor.*

KATHLEEN DICKENSON *sits at the table to finish her yoghurt.* NURSE SHEILA *leaves frame to feed another patient and says to the* WARD CLEANER *who is under the table cleaning up* KATHLEEN DICKENSON's *spilled yoghurt:*

SHEILA [BD 1a]

Oo, our Kath likes her food!

WARD CLEANER [BD 1b]

It's remarkable how they all eat!

SHEILA [BD 2, 3a]

Odd, how men all end up needing,
more than women do . . .

WARD CLEANER (*Voice over*) [BD 3b]

. . . Spoon feeding!

SHEILA (*Voice over*) [BD 4a]

But then isn't that men!

(JOHN TENNISON *enters with a plate of meat stew intended for*
MATHEW PAUL. *He places the plate on the table.*)

JOHN TENNISON [BD 4b, 5, 6]

. . . though some aren't admitting defeat.
Like Mathew Paul . . . who'll soon forget
what a fork's used for, but not yet . . .
. . proud he still can manage his meat.

CHOIR [BMW 3, 4]

All his soul says '*Go away, go away!*'
To the blizzard worsening every day.

[BMW 1–4]

Two more months of mealtimes left for Mathew Paul
before the fork he fights with makes its final fall.

And Mathew Paul he kept his pride, kept his pride,
for two more months of mealtimes, then he died.

(*The last note is cut off by* MATHEW PAUL'*s fork falling from his
hand onto his plate. The sounds of a hospital tug, like the distant
gusts of a blizzard.*)

INT. WHERNSIDE WARD ENTRANCE CORRIDOR, DAY

The face of MARIA TOBIN *appears at the glass panel of the door of
Whernside Ward, gazing down the long corridor.*

35. INT. LONG CORRIDOR LEADING TO WHERNSIDE WARD, DAY
The THERAPIST *arrives on another visit to Whernside Ward, this ti* *for a session with* MURIEL PRIOR.

36. INT. WHERNSIDE WARD, DAY
MURIEL PRIOR, *supported by nurses* IRENE KIRK *and* SHEILA BROWN, *shuffles slowly towards a table.*

CHOIR (*Voice over*) [BMW 1–4]
  Muriel Prior's scarcely able still to walk,
  only says 'I love you' if and when she'll talk.

  Two names though are still entwined, still entwined
  in a loveknot deep in Muriel's mind.

37. INT. WHERNSIDE WARD, NURSING OFFICE, DAY
A NURSE (*who will sing the Song of the Bride III*) *writes on the na* *board the name of* MURIEL PRIOR

38. INT. WHERNSIDE WARD, DAY
The THERAPIST *sits close to* MURIEL PRIOR. *She writes on a pad* *names* MURIEL *and* JIM.

THERAPIST (*Pointing to first name*)
  What does this say Muriel?
MURIEL PRIOR
  Muriel.
  (THERAPIST *now points to the name* JIM *written on the pad.*)
MURIEL PRIOR (*Reading*)
  Jim!
  My husband!
  (*Soundtrack: the first two notes of the Song of the Bride III – ba* *on the Therapist's 'Daisy, Daisy', Dacre, arr. Muldowney – seen* *both to attract* MURIEL PRIOR'*s attention and to activate the 6 .* *... of the Whernside Ward door's access code: 6288.*)

39. WHERNSIDE WARD ENTRANCE CORRIDOR, DAY
Close-up of a finger pressing the final digits ...8...8 of the access co

5288. *The …8…8 is synchronized to the third and fourth notes of the Song of the Bride III.*

A blue nurse's uniform passes through the frame. The door opens.

40. INT. LONG HOSPITAL CORRIDOR, DAY
The NURSE *emerges as the young bride* MURIEL PRIOR.

Close-up of the young MURIEL PRIOR'*s eyes which remind us of the characteristic eye movement of the old* MURIEL PRIOR. *She sings and is revealed in all her wedding finery, and she walks down the long corridor singing the Song of the Bride III.*

On the line: 'but me the bride stays locked outside/and can't walk into Whernside Ward', the BRIDE *turns towards the door of Whernside Ward, and is seen in reverse angle through the mesh of the window of the door out of the Ward, framed by the cream-coloured door. To the right of the window a blue and white circular sign reads* FIRE DOOR KEEP SHUT.

After the lines: 'Muriel! Muriel! Some moments when I call/I feel you hear me but mostly not at all', the BRIDE *makes a characteristic eye movement left where she sees through the open fanlight of a corridor window gusts of the blizzard of confetti and forgetfulness.*

Cut to: close-up of the bouquet of fresh anenomes, on which a few flakes of confetti fall. As she moves out of frame we cut back to her older self on Whernside Ward.

THE SONG OF THE BRIDE III
Muriel Prior

Mem'ry! Mem'ry! There's no access code or key
into memories old Muriel shared with me,
but something I started saying
survives until today in
her 'I love you', that's when us two
are together as we should be.

(Muriel! Muriel! Behind those big blue eyes
mem'ry's dying before the person dies.
It's like old Mother Hubbard
with memory as the cupboard.
It's been stripped bare of what was there
though you'd stocked up a life's supplies.)

Muriel! Muriel! We should have a great hoard
of life's best moments gathered with love and stored.
We should have a mem'ry brimming
with scenes with us and Jim in
but me the bride stays locked outside
and can't walk into Whernside Ward.

Muriel! Muriel! Some moments when I call
I feel you hear me but mostly not at all.
There's a blizzard now dividing
the day you were a bride in
from these you'll spend until the end
watching burying flurries fall.

(Muriel! Muriel! Sometimes when I call
I feel you hear me but mostly not at all.
Your steady blue-eyed gaze is
through blizzards to black daisies,
where once there grew of every hue,
life as full as a flower stall.)

24

Muriel! Muriel! I'm the Muriel who wed
but your memories of being me are fled.
You've forgotten when you married
the anenomes you carried,
the sad thing is, anenomes
stand unnoticed above your head.

(*Getting quieter.*)

Muriel! Muriel! My voice in your ear grows less,
fading into the storm of forgetfulness.
If life gave you back tomorrow
our memories, joy and sorrow,
not just the best, but all the rest,
would you want to relive them . . . ?

MURIEL PRIOR (*The resident in Whernside Ward*)
        . . . YES!

41. ROSTRUM CAMERA SHOT

Rostrum camera shot of the wedding photograph of MURIEL PRIOR *with her husband Jim. The bride carries a bouquet identical to the arrangement of anenomes in the ward.*

The photograph is seen through the mesh of the window of the door out of Whernside Ward, framed by the cream-coloured door. To the right of the window a blue and white circular sign reads FIRE DOOR KEEP SHUT. *The camera pulls focus from the window mesh to the photograph of the married couple (cf. number 22).*

42. INT. WHERNSIDE WARD, DAY

MURIEL PRIOR *seated in a blue chair beneath the arrangement of plastic anenomes, as if hearing some verses of the song. As the camera moves from the plastic anenomes to her face she answers the final question of the young bride* MURIEL PRIOR *with a whispered 'Yes!'*

MURIEL PRIOR (*Sync*)
'Wh . . . wh . . . what about that . . . that thing that I wanted to do?'

CHOIR
Muriel Prior's 'I love you' used to fill the air.
Now she's a nurse's memory and an empty chair.

43. INT. WHERNSIDE WARD NURSING OFFICE, DAY

CHOIR [BMW 1, 2]
Muriel braves the blizzard with her big blue eyes.
In a few more weeks, though, Muriel Prior dies.
(*Cut to: the plastic anenomes on a shelf above the blue chair in the ward where Muriel Prior always sits. Behind these shelves the* NURSE *who sang the Song of the Bride III enters from a maroon door marked* FEMALE TOILET, *wearing white rubber gloves and carrying a yellow plastic waste sack. She stops to remove her glove and as she does so the camera pans down from the anenomes to the now empty blue chair.*

26

Camera pans down the board of residents' names. We hear the
CHOIR *begin to sing.*)

[BMW 1–4]
For the men and women written on this board
Death's got the only door-code out of Whernside Ward.

And till Rene Parker died, Rene died,
her husband's weekly kisses consoled his bride.

[BMW 1–4]
Only eight more kisses then he'll lose his dear,
swept off in the blizzard where brides disappear.

Eight more weeks for Mathew Paul, who says GO AWAY
to the blizzard worsening every day.

[BMW 1, 2]
Though the blizzard's blowing, right until the last
he'll sing 'Daisy, Daisy' through the stormy blast.

44. INT. WHERNSIDE WARD, DAY
*Cut to: a pianist on the ward piano playing 'Daisy, Daisy'. The
camera tracks to discover the* THERAPIST *with* MATHEW PAUL *in
mid duet:*
    . . . It won't be a stylish marriage,
    I can't afford a carriage,
    But you'll look sweet upon the seat
    of a bicycle made for two.
    etc.
    (*Cut to: the sneakered feet of* MURIEL ALLEN *leaving the frame.*)

45. INT. WHERNSIDE WARD, ENTRANCE CORRIDOR, DAY
The face of MARIA TOBIN *appears at the meshed glass panel of
Whernside Ward door, gazing down the long hospital corridor.*
    She sees RICHARD MUTTONCHOPS, *the hospital entertainer, who
enters Whernside Ward with his banjo.*

46. INT. WHERNSIDE WARD, DAY
IRENE CLEMENTS *in her fractured English signals the arrival of*
RICHARD MUTTONCHOPS.

MUTTONCHOPS *begins to play 'Oh You Beautiful Doll' to* MARIA
TOBIN, *who is hand in hand with the* NURSE, JOYCE MCINTOSH.

MUTTONCHOPS
　　Oh! You beautiful doll, you great big beautiful doll!
　　Let . . . me put my arms about you,
　　I could never live without you.
　　Oh! You beautiful doll, you great big beautiful doll!
　　If you ever leave me how my heart will ache,
　　I want to hug you, but I fear you'd break,
　　Oh, oh, oh, oh, Oh you beautiful doll!
　　(MARIA TOBIN *dances in response, but when she sings she utters the
　　familiar 'one note out of* Butterfly'. *She says to* MUTTONCHOPS,
　　'Well, you are *a beautiful doll!' and continues dancing.*

　　　　MUTTONCHOPS *serenades seated residents, most of whom show
　　little response until he reaches* IRENE CLEMENTS *sitting with the*
　　NURSE ANGELA FIELDING, *who has her arm around* IRENE's
　　shoulder, beating time to the music.

　　　　IRENE CLEMENTS *begins to sing along with* MUTTONCHOPS,
　　*though the words are incomprehensible. None the less the energy and
　　tone of the rendition remind us that* IRENE *spent many years as a
　　pub crooner.*

　　　　MUTTONCHOPS *passes on to serenade* KATHLEEN DICKENSON,
　　*who is cleaning a central heating radiator with her fingers. At the
　　sound of the music she turns and begins to sway in time to the song.
　　It is as if she is moving to the rhythm of and reclaiming the Song of
　　the Bride II her young self sang in the corridor. It seems that she's
　　'glad she's still Kath and alive'.)*

47. INT. WHERNSIDE WARD, DAY. CLOSE TO CHRISTMAS
MARIA TOBIN, *swathed in green Christmas tinsel as if she were
wrapped in furs for the opera, utters her familiar one note.*
　　*The ward is being prepared for Christmas. A box of tinsel
decorations and Christmas-tree baubles is deposited on a table. Five
nurses begin to sort out the decorations and decorate the Christmas tree.
They are* MARIA BOVINO, SHEILA BROWN, JOYCE MCINTOSH,
AUDREY ROBINSON *and* LIZ YOUNG.

SHEILA BROWN [BD 1–4a]
  I bet some memories'll stir, once we've put lights on our tree.
  Bound to get some mem'ries stirring
  with gold and frankincense and myrrh in.
  Bound to stir up a few.

LIZ YOUNG [BD 4b]
                    I hope that's how it'll be!

JOYCE MCINTOSH [BD 5, 6]
  When the kids sing carols, though I could be wrong,
  I bet a few ours'll sing along.

SHEILA BROWN [BD 7]
  Christmas *always* sets some memories free!

LIZ YOUNG [BD 1–3]
  Yes, for someone like you, without Alzheimer's, that's true!
  (LIZ YOUNG *sees* KATHLEEN DICKENSON *bustling about the
  ward cleaning near another Christmas tree.*)
  Christmas can't have too much meaning
  When you spend all year spring-cleaning!

MARIA BOVINO
  Our Maria'll give a wobbly warble or two.
  We might just get carols out of Mathew Paul,
  a tune from Irene,

LIZ YOUNG
                    . . . but from most, damn all!

SHEILA BROWN (*Voice over*)
  O if only something of Christmas gets through!

8. INT. WHERNSIDE WARD NURSING OFFICE, DAY
NURSE (MARIA BOVINO) *leads* MARIA TOBIN *to the Nursing Office
board with residents' names which in the lower right hand corner
reads:* CHRISTMAS 1992, MUSIC, ST MARY'S SCHOOL.

MARIA BOVINO
  What does that say, Maria?

MARIA TOBIN
  Chris . . . mas . . . *la musica!* . . . *Santa Maria!*

29

CHOIR OF SAINT MARY'S SCHOOL (*Soundtrack*)
> In the bleak mid-winter, frosty winds made moan,
> earth stood hard as iron, water like a stone;
> snow had fallen, snow on snow, snow on snow,
> in the bleak mid-winter, long ago.
>
> What can I give him, poor as I am?
> If I were a shepherd, I would bring a lamb;
> if I were a wise man I would do my part,
> yet what I can I give him – give my heart.

49. INT. WHERNSIDE WARD, DAY

The CHOIR OF SAINT MARY'S SCHOOL *is singing the carol to the assembled residents and some of their relatives.* MRS BENFORD, *the wife of a resident* HARRY BENFORD, *is sitting between him and* IRENE CLEMENTS, *who is delivering a characteristically garbled address to a* WARD CLEANER, CHRISTINE DAVEY. MRS BENFORD, *thinking that Irene's conversation is disturbing the carol, begins to conduct* IRENE *in the rhythm of the carol, and succeeds towards the end of the verse in inducing* IRENE *to join in the tune, if not with recognizable words.*

The camera then pans from MRS LEAROYD, *wife of resident* DONALD LEAROYD, *holding his hand, through the gathered residents and comes to a halt on* MARIA TOBIN *sitting with nurse* IRENE KIRK.

Cut to MURIEL ALLEN, *former hospital therapist, whose songless but obsessively rhythmical presence haunts the performance of the carol.*

Cut to the face of MARIA TOBIN *at the glass panel of Whernside Ward Door, gazing down the long hospital corridor. She sees a procession of three brides: herself,* KATHLEEN DICKENSON *and* MURIEL PRIOR.

The THREE BRIDES *begin to sing the Song of the Bride IV.*

50. INT. LONG HOSPITAL CORRIDOR, NIGHT

The THREE BRIDES *process slowly down the darkened corridor until they disappear and* MARIA TOBIN *is left gazing down the long corridor that seems to lead onward and onward and onward towards oblivion and forgetfulness. The long empty hospital corridor finally mixes to a long fire-break in a forest of forgotten Christmases.*

THE SONG OF THE BRIDE IV
Trio

CHOIR [BMW 1–4]
  All three brides of Whernside . . .
MARIA
                                   Maria . . .
MURIEL
                                              Muriel . . .
KATHLEEN
                                                       Kath.
CHOIR
  Who once walked the aisle now walk a stormy path.
KATHLEEN
  Kath . . .
MURIEL
         Muriel . . .
MARIA
                Maria . . .
CHOIR
                       They've all lost their ways
  bearing through the blizzard withering bouquets,
MURIEL [DD 1–4]
  turned to daisies, their petals black and strewn,
  strewn on paths where carols all lose their tune.
  Though the music keeps on playing,
  the notes won't stop decaying . . .
MARIA [Puccini]
  Though the music keeps on playing
  the notes won't stop decaying.
KATHLEEN [BD 4]
  Lost with black daisy bouquets, in the burying blizzard of
  days.
  (*The corridor is empty. The sound of the hospital tug, like the gust of
  a blizzard, becomes almost tempestuous.*)

31

Mix to:

51. EXT. A FIRE-BREAK IN A FIR PLANTATION, DAY
The camera begins to track past fir tree after fir tree, and discovers a dark gap in which can be glimpsed the fluttering remnants of a wedding dress.

CHOIR (*Voice over*) [BMW 1–4]
    Through these firs oblivion's blizzards blow and moan,
    snuffing every Christmas they have ever known.

    In the forest mem'ries blur, mem'ries blur
    and the lost lose contact with the brides they were.

    [BMW 1, 2]
    If we could give them voices, we would hear them say:
    Gather all your mem'ries, savour every day.

    And the bride who wore this glove, wore this glove
    bids us all remember songs and love.

    (*The white elbow-length kid glove worn by* MARIA TOBIN *is wound around the base of a tree. The blizzard of forgetfulness begins. A heart-shaped flake of confetti falls into the open palm of the glove. The blizzard of forgetfulness intensifies and obliterates the glove in drifts of confetti. Intense flurries blow among the firs.*)

52. EXT. WHERNSIDE WARD GREEN FIRE DOOR, DAY
Through the blizzard of confetti and forgetfulness, and the sounds of the hospital tug, now like a threatening storm, the face of MARIA TOBIN *appears at the glass panel of the green fire door.*

53. INT. WHERNSIDE WARD, DAY
MURIEL ALLEN *swings the curtains across the frame as the blizzard sounds from the hospital tug seems to enter the ward itself.*
    Various faces of residents who hear the blizzard destroying their memories.

MURIEL ALLEN *keeps swaying the curtain as she did at the beginning of the film.*

The camera pans from the face of DOREEN MITCHELL *up to a plastic arrangement of carnations, but this time there is no transformation into the resident as young bride. The blizzard intensifies.*

4. INT. WHERNSIDE WARD, ENTRANCE CORRIDOR, NIGHT

MARIA TOBIN *hovers around the Whernside Ward door, trying the handle, brushing her fingers over the access code security pad without understanding its function. Her hand passes over the blue and white circular sign that reads* FIRE DOOR KEEP SHUT.

MARIA TOBIN (*Sync*)
Fire door *kept* shut.

5. INT. LONG HOSPITAL CORRIDOR, NIGHT

The face of MARIA TOBIN *appears at the meshed glass panel of the Whernside Ward door.*

MARIA TOBIN (*Sync*)
Goodbye darling, thank you very much, don't go far.

6. INT. WHERNSIDE WARD ENTRANCE CORRIDOR, NIGHT

MARIA TOBIN's *point-of-view: a glow of blue and yellow through the meshed glass. The camera pulls focus from the wire of the mesh to discover a hospital tug laden with blue and yellow waste sacks. A blue one nearest the glass panel has a white label which reads* GENERAL WASTE.

The tug pulls away with the sound we have associated throughout the film with the blizzard of forgetfulness. It proceeds down the long darkened corridor.

Close-up of yellow and blue plastic waste sacks with one of the blue sacks bursting open to scatter flakes of confetti in the wake of the hospital tug.

The tug passes through frame still scattering confetti in its wake.

A scattering of still flakes of confetti.

The sound of the hospital tug recedes into the distance.

The sound of the four numbers 6–2–8–8 being pressed. The sound of

33

Whernside Ward door opening, creaking closed, and slamming shut.

The scattered flakes of confetti jump in the gust from the doors and resettle into stillness.

Soundtrack: over the disappearing hospital tug, the voice of the young MARIA TOBIN *is heard singing the lines from* Madama Butterfly:

Ah, love me a little,

Oh just a very little,

As you would love a baby.

'Tis all that I ask for . . .

The sound of the Whernside Ward door closing cuts off the aria in mid-flow.